Anatomy of a Broken Heart

Aubrey Ann

to my children
the lights
my loves
i love you
forevermore

Anatomy of a Broken Heart
© 2025 Aubrey Ann
All rights reserved.

No part of this publication may be reproduced, distributed, or transmitted in any form or by any means, electronic or mechanical, including photocopying, recording, or by any information storage and retrieval system, without the prior written permission of the author, except in the case of brief quotations in reviews or critical articles.

This is a work of creative nonfiction and poetry. Names and identifying details may have been changed. Any resemblance to actual persons, living or deceased, is purely coincidental.

Published by Aubrey Ann
ISBN: 9781764186315
Printed by authorised printing partners worldwide.

This collection contains themes of heartbreak and trauma that may be distressing to some readers.

Pathology Report

Preliminary Postmortem   9

The Truth and The Fight	10
Game	11
WCS	12
It Begins.	13
Shame and Hope	14
August Entry	15
Sixteen Days, Scattered Thoughts & Sixteen Questions	16
BABYGIRL.	17
Pretty is a Lie	18
Chessmate	19
Destroy Me Later	20
Pit	21
The Cost Of Love	22
Hold The Line	23
One Am In The Morning	25
Homicide a Heart	26
LOVEHATE.	27
Ghost Driver	28
White Flag	29
The Wardeness + The Witness	30
His Fault	31
You Don't Deserve It.	32
I'm Sick Of My Pillow Smelling Like You	33
Dreamer.	34
The Aches Of Loneliness	35
November & December	36
Quarry	37
Void	38
Probably Desperation	39
Chasm	40
Fool's Note	41
Flicker	42
Pieces	43
The Eighth Of Stupid March	44
Burn Everything	45
Last Story	46
April Fool	47
No One Will Ever Be Enough For You	48
GAMBLER	49
Permanent	50

May	51
Impending Death?	52
You're Not Welcome Anymore	53
Cursed Spotify	54
Premonition	55
TRUCE	56
June	57
3 Weeks And 4 Days Of The Truce	58
Happy Birthday To Me	59
Or You Don't	60
Preparation	61
Chore	62
I Tended The Gardens, They Bloomed	63
Blank	64
Through	65
[Insert Title]	66
Red	67
Five-Ten	68
How?	69
I Truly Don't Want To Do This	70
Aubrey Ann	71
Two-Seven	72
12:01AM	73
December	74
Unveiled Affair	75
?What I lost in the fire?	
What I gained from the fire?	76
Shatter	77
January	78
Embers Linger	79
Fated	80
Lost Note	81
Admit The Truth, Set Me Free	82
Cursed	83
Answers	84
Reality	85
The 22nd	86
Haunted	87
Make It Make Sense	88
Mirrors, Smoke, Fire	89
Fateful Delusion	90
I'm Wondering…	91
Sea Through	92

Virtuosity	93
When I Was…	94
Burn Off	95
Romanticised Fabrication	96
Play Stupid Games, Win Stupid Prizes	97
Modern Lust Story	98
Me Villain, You Hero	99
Just the Two of Us, Just the Three of Us	100
I'll Forget You, But I'll Never Forgive	101
Retribution	102
Never, EVER, Again	103
Modern Courtship Revolution	104
Alternate Reality	105
The 26th of [Stupid] May	106
Postmortem Withdrawn	**107**

Preliminary Postmortem

A note before the dissection begins…

This book was never meant to be a book.
Never, ever, meant to be published.

It was a collection of scribbled outpourings of anguished feelings in notebooks through salted teardrops, letters penned in heartache and frustration never to be posted, texts written and deleted, voice notes on long drives, diary entries in the dead of the night, words never said aloud because they hurt too much.

It was grief and confusion, anger and desperation, frustration and pain, softness and surrender and sadness, transferred onto pages because my heart needed somewhere safe to land.

I didn't write this to be understood; I wrote it so I could understand myself.

But, if you've ever been where I've been, if you've ever stayed too long, hoped too hard, ignored every red flag, put your heart on the line for potential because you wanted the dream more than the truth, then this is for you.

These are all the pieces I wanted to bury, the poems I was scared to share. But here they are.

And maybe in reading this collection of poetry and paragraphs, you'll feel less alone in whatever chapter of heartbreak you're surviving right now.

Because we survive it.

We always do.

- Aubrey Ann

August 2022

The Truth and The Fight

If I'm not on your mind, I don't exist
My self-worth lies in a stranger's effort
And then, I have to admit all the breaks
The scratches, burns, cuts, scars and bruises
I look fine…
But it's all there, scattered on my skin
Tiger's stripes, leopard's spots

I walk around, a zombie
But it's the other way
I'm acting cool
I'm being normal
I can handle it all
You'd never know
You'd never know what's under my skin
In my chest, my stomach
Surging through my veins

The self-deprecation
The shame
The frustration
The battle
The wars inside

All for the
Eager desperate desire
Despondent minuscule attention
Any despairing affection

August 2022

Game

Are you the reddest piece of cloth
Or just emotionally broken, so you can't be
Even the most averagely expected respectful person

And then there's you…

Always hiding in the wings
Ready to descend
Self- proclaimed saviour
With your broken vows
Your accidental lies
And still, you do nothing

See their actions
Stop, and see their actions
Not your feelings
Not your made up fantasies

No one is coming to save you
You have to learn
You have to do it yourself

I hate the fucking game
I hate this game

August 2022

WCS

1.
    Why do I feel the need to fix them?
    Why can't I just fix myself?
    Why did they all have to,
    Break me in the first place?

2.
    Every single person
    Stole parts of my soul
    I want it back
    I want my innocence back
    I want my childhood back
    I want my life to be mine
    Not what they did to me
    Which made me do things to myself

It Begins.

August 2022

Shame and Hope

I was going to rip out the pain
And throw it away
Hide the shame
Pretend I didn't make the mistake/s

But that isn't how to be whole
And I want to show up whole

I literally… legitimately
Feel that I manifested us
Manifested you
It's everything I ever wanted
Communication
Desire
Effort
Friendship
Humour
Maturity

It's all I ever wanted

August 2022

Is it sad that I'm surprised he just wants to spend time with me that isn't all in bed? That he actually likes me, likes spending time with me? I think the only other person that actually liked me, for who I actually am, was my first love. And just then, when I listened to a sad song that reminded me of heartbreak, I realise this could hurt so fucking bad. How do I protect myself? Can you even stop from falling?

September 2022

Sixteen Days, Scattered Thoughts & Sixteen Questions

What a fucking roller coaster
How can communicating be this hard?
When it's so honest?
Or is it a sign that it's not honest?

What are my needs?
How do I meet them?
Who helps to fulfil them?

Why do I give it all away?

Every. Single. Time.

Am I blinded by lust?
Did I turn the flags from blood red to blush?
What can you see that I can't?

Because I can make an entire fairytale novel
Fit inside a realistic reality with anyone
But, especially with you

Are you really worth it?
Or the very first to treat me with bare minimum?
I think I'm older
I think I'm wiser
I think I did the other times too?

How many of today's tears were over you?
Should I let anyone have any?

Am I going crazy… already?

September 2022

BABYGIRL.

Screaming and crying
Abandoned and alone
Desperate and aching
She is longing
She wants it all

Love, Safety, Security
Attention, Affection, Acceptance

She looks to them
To make her whole
Makes it dull with any haze
Anything to numb the days

She says yes, but means no
She gives it all away, any takers?
She betrays herself
In every way
On any day

She exists in the pain
Body suffering
Soul anguished
A constant battle
To win no wars

The light creeps in
Painfully bright

The battle scars finally put to use
If she didn't have them
She couldn't bear this

September 2022

Pretty is a Lie

Reality is settling in

It's not as pretty as it was

But being pretty isn't being beautiful

So, does that mean we could still be beautiful?

September 2022

Chessmate

I don't want to be alone
I want to share my time and my love
But you can't take it, you won't

One of us will have to break it
Long game, countless moves

Fucking checkmate

Will it be Queen?
Will it be King?

September 2022

Destroy Me Later

We have a true connection
But your uncertainty
About what you want
And what is in your future
Influenced how you treated me

You thought it didn't
You thought you hid it

But… I felt it

And it hurt, so deeply

Sad to end this
Proud to put myself first

The first time I've ever
Put a boundary up
I deserve better
I'm worth more

I'm worth surety
I'm worth commitment
I'm worth falling for

I don't want to miss you
I already do

But I have to hurt myself now
So you don't destroy me later

September 2022

Pit

The pit in my stomach won't go away
I guess I can be grateful for the tears
I'm now able to have control over
My mind is a pendulum
Swinging between the heart and the mind

The mind says
You're amazing and strong
This was a million percent the right decision
That if it was meant for me
Meant to be
It wouldn't be like this
So now you can be sad, move on, learn the lesson

The heart says
What if we never feel this again?
It was magic, rare, extraordinary
Or was it?
Was it just a mirage in my heart?

I want him to regret it
I want him to be aching for me
I want him to feel so much regret and pain
Come like a white knight to claim
His prize and take me into forever

But… I sit still, pit in my stomach

September 2022

The Cost Of Love

I'm scared that
The hold you have on me is eternal
Like the gentle way
Your elegant hands
Enclose my neck
Is that what you're remembering
I think you're confused
You said hello…
But am I just being used

Is my power back enough
I never thought that giving my body
So beautifully intertwined
Would bring me my power

The others aren't like you
But I've got to force myself to try
I can't let you put me on layaway
I'm worth both
Premium price, immediate payment
You'll have to pay up
If you want it all back

Love costs
It always has
You pay

In bravery and in fear
In joy and in magic
No drug does it better

But you don't regret it
Do you?

September 2022

Hold The Line

You messaged again
After 11
I missed it
Grateful
Only for 20 minutes
I reply

But I realise
This is why
No contact

You're not saying you miss me
And you want me
And it is all a mistake
And you
Unequivocally
Need me in your life
And you're all in

Instead

You're wishing
You left something
At my house
Or in my room
So you can be
In my bed

I have to make sure

I hold the line

If you can't choose yourself, how will anyone else?

One Am In The Morning

*I'm mad now. Furious. You came on so strong and it felt **so** real. How the fuck did I not see it wasn't real? I'm not a child anymore. <u>I kept **every** version of the **delusion** going.</u> Every excuse. He is hurt. He is scared. He needs time. I can show him, I can make it better, I can heal it. He is unsure. He is confused. He is scared. He likes me so much, the fear is driving the behaviour. I don't want to give you one single more tear. But I think they're for me now. I'm ruminating, all the what if's, all the why's? Trying to see what I missed. What I can do better next time. I don't want to become bitter. But I do want love. I'm so tired. So I say to myself, you can cry a little more, just tonight and tomorrow. But then you're done. Done. It's one am in the morning.*

September 2022

Homicide a Heart

You entangled me in a false start of true love
And when you discarded me
Leaving me nothing more than a shell
It was so much easier than you'll ever admit
Because your ego is more valuable to you than the truth

Save your face
Save your pride
Save your reputation
You don't have to pay the price, so it's okay
Does it make you selfish?
Or a cunning narcissist?

It wasn't right person, wrong timing
My timing is fine
You're the wrong person
For anyone

You took and took from me
I gave and gave
But you knew, for sure you knew
You were going to let go
And watch me fall
And crash
And burn
Decimated

And the final act of the execution?

You handed me the knife
Indulgent eyes watching
A vindicated smile unfurled from your lips
As you compelled me to make the cut

September 2022

LOVEHATE.

My heart is heavy
A boundless melancholy
I want to be angry
I want to be bursting with rage

The line between love and hate
Is so fragile and delicate
I'm begging
I'm desperate

I have to hate you
Because the truth is
I love you

September 2022

Ghost Driver

If it's not a lie

It's deeply painful

I don't understand

How can you want me so bad it hurts

But let your ghosts take the wheel

October 2022

White Flag

I Surrender.

We're Magnets.

October 2022

The Wardeness + The Witness

Incite a deliberate drought
The starvation of love
Let it all wither and wane
Until it is dust enough for the wind

Every passing minute
A torturous lifetime

It would have been easier
If one of us lit the match
Burned it all
Ember to ash

Water couldn't save us from the fire
But it could revive us from the drought

You decided a merciless drought
Then watered it again… and again… and again

Now my threadbare heart
Is in turmoil
Because you chose me to be both

The Wardeness and The Witness

He said I'm perfect, he said all the things.
That it was his fault. And it was.

October 2022

You Don't Deserve It.

You don't deserve it,
But you're the only person I want to call.

You don't deserve it,
But you're the only person I want to kiss.

You don't deserve it,
But you're the only person I want to date.

You don't deserve it,
But you're the only person I want to love.

You don't deserve it,
But you're the only person I want.

You don't deserve it.

October 2022

I'm Sick Of My Pillow Smelling Like You

I'm not changing the sheets again.
I'm not erasing your energy again.

I'll never water myself down again.
To make me more palatable,
Easier to swallow, to accept, to love.

You don't get the highs without the lows,
You don't get to consume my love,
Without accepting and respecting my pain.

When has addiction ever ended well?
Only when you eradicate it from your life.

No more turmoil.
I want the safe, the sweet, the secure,
The calm.

October 2022

Dreamer.

His lips are lush and soft and kissable
He never tires of me
Always wants to learn more
Hear my stories, ask my opinions

He can't stand to see me cry
His body desires me persistently

He loves my mind, my thoughts
My dreams, my goals
My expressions, my mannerisms

He is patient, and kind, and fiercely protective

He doesn't hurt me, not at all, not ever

He is sure he wants love
But he is more sure
He wants to love me

eternally – hopeful – manifesting – dream – wishes

October 2022

The Aches of Loneliness

Ruptures out from the depths of my heart
Ricochets through my chest
Remnants felt to my extremities

They say you can heal it yourself
They say you can sew the tattered shreds of flesh
Watch it bond together and see the scars fade

But they never tell you how…

So
I breathe
Every breath
Shredding
Ripping
My pain seeps out
Escaping
Through my words, my eyes, my mind

I am begging
Any relief
Desperately

I don't want this pain to become my comfort

NOVEMBER

                Back, Forth, Pain, *Heartache*

DECEMBER

                Back, Forth, Pain, *Heartbreak*

January 2023

Quarry

What did we do?
What have I done?

You cannot play pretend
Make it less than it is

You're forcing me
This isn't what I want
I already told you
You already know
You didn't ask if I'm okay

It was fun
But it was fleeting
Fraudulent delight
I'm left feeling anxious
Worthless

But I still want you

I don't know what I'm doing anymore

February 2023

Void

I fill your cup
You don't fill mine

I'm still alone
I can't ask for anything

I said I would wait
Until it doesn't feel good

I don't feel good

Unwanted
Undesired
Used
Undervalued

February 2023

Probably Desperation

Trying to hold on
Trying to be patient

It's probably desperation though
Not love

This isn't the next love story
The ones people like me melt over
An enmeshed story of reality and magic

You're not getting over the line
You can't
And you've chosen not to
Both are true

I can't feel like this
I won't
I deserve better

Worthy

February 2023

Chasm

I'm disappointed and hurt,
That I'm going to be disappointed and hurt.

Why am I still holding on?
What am I even holding onto?

I wanted to get over it while I was still in it.
Then when it ended, it would be done.

That means feeling the pain,
And it hurts,
So badly.

The deepest chasm,

    Vast,

       Endless.

You would have to choose to love me,
So intently that,
The chasm closed up and filled in.

I know you won't.
You know you won't.

Disappointed, is worse than lonely.

Expected disappointment, worse still.

You're the fool that already knows.

February 2023

Flicker

I can hardly believe
That still
After all the pain
There is a spark
Flickering inside me

Hoping
Wishing
Thinking

The grand gesture will arrive

But it didn't
Instead
It's done.

February 2023

Pieces

I don't want to search

For pieces of us

In every new person I meet

For the rest of forever

the eighth of stupid march

March 2023

Burn Everything

You're gone
You left
Discarded us
Every broken imperfect memory

You could find me if you wanted to
You could change your mind if you wanted to
You could love me if you wanted to

You've never done anything like this before

You're just fine
Just perfect
Free
Relieved

I'm not free or relieved or fine

Fuelled by the actions
That made our good memories
Into disgusting lies
Deception

I think our bridge has finally burned

March 2023

Last Story

The story pens itself
Turbulent twists
Triggering turns
Fighting and gasping
For just one full breath
Just one

And even though you're the one drowning me
And your ornate hands encircle my neck
I can only resurface and inhale
When I'm with you

Reality is never as peaceful as the dreams in your mind

When you combine the intensity of
Everything we share
Everything we are
Everything we've ever been
Everything we want to be

I've only ever lost what I've loved
You've only ever lost what you've loved

But if we don't cut it off
Discarded ghostly pasts
The only proof we've ever known
It'll never feel real
It'll be the last story we ever have to tell

April 2023

I wish this was April Fools on April Fools, but I am the only Fool.

If I write this down, it's all going to be real. And some of it I don't want to be real. Last night took me back to some really fucked up places. I never want to feel like that again. Trapped, Invisible, Ignored. How can you watch me cry and not snap out of your cruelness and comfort me? YOU wanted ME! You BEGGED me! You CONVINCED me to give you yet another chance! Said that you loved me, and it all made sense to get to this because we are meant to be together. It took me days to give in and believe you because I didn't want to be hurt by you, again, AGAIN. Then as soon as I agree you start making sure I'm walking on eggshells and you're twisting everything, and I don't understand why. Why does it never feel enough? I think I've always felt like this in relationships. Being triggered doesn't mean you get to be cruel. Why don't you want me more? Because now you have me so it's boring for you now? Now we committed to this you have a green light to treat me as awful as you possibly can. I don't actually know who you are or what you want.

Right now, you're a liar
Right now, you're being cruel
Right now, you're being unfair
You are literally about to lose me and you don't care
You push me aside for time alone
You push me aside for work
You push me aside for friends
I can't be mixed with any parts of your life
So where does that leave time or effort for me
I can't fucking do this
It's fucking crazy
You're ruining this
You.

April 2023

no one will ever be enough for you

There was a time
Only days ago
I hadn't been lied to
Not in this way
I couldn't quite understand
What that truly felt like

It doesn't matter
Not one tiny bit
If you meant it or not
The facts stay the same
The proof is in your lying
Your words are nothing

Barely enough time to understand
And now I'm just alone, again
Feeling like I'll be forever crying
I couldn't have given any less
And I couldn't have given you any more

I offered you the entire universe
All the stars in the sky
I scoured countless shores for eternity
To find and give to you
The perfect grain of sand

It still wasn't enough

No one will ever be enough

April 2023

GAMBLER

The chance I took

The trust I gave to you

Meant I lost the trust

I had in myself

And you don't deserve that

April 2023

Permanent

I know in my deepest truths
That this has brought me
The most critical invaluable lessons
But it doesn't make it hurt any less

The damage
I can tell already
It's **permanent**

Meanwhile
I know how to treat the wounds
Heal the disease
And I even know
How to soften the scars

I swear
I won't have to learn this lesson again
I won't have to heal this affliction again

One day, a long time away
I might even reminisce with gratitude

I deserve that kind of resolve
That depth of peace

May 2023

I thought I lost it all

But I had no idea

What was coming

In May

June 2023

Impending Death?

I wish I didn't see every side of everyone's story
I wish especially I didn't see your side of our story

Because I just want peace and freedom

I pray at night to wake up
And not love you

I've never endured a pain like this before
It won't stop coming at me
Thick
Fast
Assaulting
Piercing
Is death coming?
And the universe needs me to learn
Before I'm gone

They call it a broken heart
Because you feel it
As real
As a real
Broken heart

June 2023

You're not welcome anymore

I'd do anything for you
For love
For our love
But your love
Is an actionless love
A faithless love
Bound love
Kept love

I won't let myself fight for it anymore
I can't keep witnessing
You not fighting for me
And I can't comprehend how you stood
And watched me walk out the door
No, you pushed me out the door
So many times
And then another

I repeat to myself
Over and over

You've only got yourself to blame

And I do

Because you've shown me so many times
What you are capable of

And I live in a precious romanticised world
And you're not welcome here anymore

June 2023

Cursed Spotify

Kind of hate it
When you share
Beautiful music
With me
Because I know
One day
Soon
It'll destroy me
To hear it
So even though
It makes me smile today
And love you more
Right now
It makes me cry
Because I know
Soon
Hearing it
Will devastate me
To my core
And beyond

June 2023

Premonition

I've done hard things
The hardest
So, if I have to I will

I'll block your number
I'll focus on me
I'll do incantations
I'll plead to the moon
I'll date nobody's
I'll heal and grow and get better

I'll desperately do all the things
They tell you to do

But I don't want to

June 2023

TRUCE

It just doesn't stop
If I let the smallest
Glimmer of hope
Seep through
The cracks in my heart
Put there by you
I start to feel
So much
More feelings than
I have ever felt before
It's overwhelming
I try to catch my breath
I try not to cry
I don't even know
And it's because I don't know
If I will be crying from
Heights of joy
Or
Depths of pain

one day in June, I write a letter to you, never to be delivered

I am so scared right now. All you've taught me that it's safe to do, is to run from you. I know you're trying, I know you have been all the other times too. I need you to understand, if we are spending time together, and I'm letting myself be <u>with</u> you, then I'm <u>in love with you</u>. I try so hard to just only let a little bit out, pack it up when you walk out the door. **Because <u>for 295 days</u>, what I know, the proof I have, is that it will end and end badly for me.** *And you know what else? It's kind of impossible to just let yourself love someone just a little bit, for a little bit of time. So, I'm terrified, because I'm here again. Overwhelmed with feelings, not knowing if I'll be crying from joy or pain. I want to be able to give you what you feel like you need. It just feels way too unsafe for me. I want to hold on as long as I can. I fight myself about it all the time. I'm not sure how it's ever going to be possible for us to get there, because we've ended up here. I see you, I see your passion and your imperfections, your magic and your humanity. And I'm here saying, what we have between us makes the real, mundane, boring, human parts of you and me and life worth the passion and love and magic we can have together. But we'd have to jump and risk it together, at the same time. We'd have to blindly trust each other and change the current pattern of 'us'. I wish I knew what you were actually feeling and thinking. I love you.*

July 2023

3 weeks and 4 days of the truce

You're supposed to make me feel happy, but I feel sad
You're supposed to make me feel safe, but I feel scared
You're supposed to make me feel loved, but I feel invisible

You tell me things you *don't* like about me, often
My piercing, my flared pants, how I'm too nice

But you don't tell me my eyes are beautifully green
Or that you love the way I want to kiss you all the time
Instead… you said that it's a lot
One Sunday you said to me
That I'm too much
You actually said that

You make sure I know we aren't officially together
I don't have dates
I don't have romance
I don't have affection
I don't have commitment
I don't have a relationship

I should leave first, I really should leave first
I wish I was strong enough to leave first

July 2023

Happy Birthday To Me

I waited
For weeks you said it
You said my birthday
So I waited
All day
All night
I waited

Sitting at the restaurant
The day is running out of time
You pay the bill
I'm forced to say
Thank You

For breaking my heart

But it's my birthday
And I can't bring myself
To bring it up
And blow it up
On my birthday

So, I keep my mouth shut
Be a good girl
Be a nice girl
Say thank you
Go to sleep

July 2023

Or you don't

You either want me, or you don't
You either want to be with me, or you don't
You either want to make me happy, or you don't

I can't let myself stay in something like this

Calling it a relationship but not treating me well
Doesn't fix anything

I don't deserve it
I should be giving my love
To someone who enjoys it
Is grateful for it
Not despises it
Or uses it

You thank me for my patience and kindness
But you don't return it
I don't deserve that either

Shutting me up
And shutting me down
Is dimming the light in me

Why would you want to do that?

August 2023

Preparation

Shave my legs
Wash my hair
Lather every inch of my body
With the best of balms
I sit on the bed
Let everything melt in
I painstakingly
Carefully
And deliberately
Choose
Every layer of clothing
Even after almost a whole year
As though there might
Maybe
Be a chance
That tonight is my one in ten
That you'll notice
And you'll care
And you'll want me
And tonight
You'll actually
Make me feel
Like you like me

August 2023

Chore

I don't feel anything from you about me

It just feels like I'm your chore

Bound by boundaries

Ruled by rules

That I somehow agreed on

August 2023

I tended the gardens, they bloomed

I built us a castle
I tended the gardens, they bloomed
I made beds, warm
I cooked meals, nurturing
With love
All my love

You
Burned it all to the ground
Demolished
You
Made me rebuild
And do it again
And again

And now
I'm supposed to make
Another castle
Another garden
Again
But you're not even really here

How can you be happy
When I'm sad
And you know
Most of my sadness
Is because of you

August 2023

Blank

I don't know how to love someone
Who has hurt me this much
And still can't and won't
Love me now

I literally don't know what to do
                        Or think
                              Or say
                                    Or feel
                                        Or be…

September 2023

The only way out is through.

September 2023

[insert title]

I don't want you anymore
You treated me worse than filth
I don't respect you
I wish I never met you
I wish I didn't give you more than a year
I wish I had ran, fast and far

I'm ashamed to say
I hope you're miserable
Regretful, sad, lonely
For the rest of your life

I'm desperate for indifference

You're a ghost in my heart
I would pay any price
For a failsafe exorcism
I wish you and your memory
Would disappear for good
For forever

Nothing is a fond memory
And you don't deserve to keep them

September 28, 2023

Something bad
Really bad
Trauma-Indirect
Life-Changing
Surgeons, the ICU and signing consent forms
Social workers and phone calls and info-sheets
Laparotomy and Arch Bars and Brain Bleeds
Constant Hums and Beeps
The machines
Convulse then suction
Convulse then suction
TBI
Conversation
Decision
Another
Will I ever go home again
Will any of us ever be the same again
How can the kids survive this
How can I do this
When I'm already broken
I have no choice

Keep

Fucking

Going

October 2023

five-ten

This time it's your birthday
You call
You don't know what's happened
I haven't been home in days, in weeks
You profess and confess
Your undying love

I'm too vulnerable to fight it
I need someone to hold me
I've never been more numb
More empty
So, I let you see me
And then I let you see me again

Everything is the biggest mess I've ever seen
My life is shattered, tattered, torn
It's not mine right now
I don't know if it ever will be again

I have to help him
You say you're going to help me
Because you care

But
It doesn't last long
Of course

October 2023

How?

How can this be?
How could God, the Universe, Whoever?
Have possibly put me here?
How?

Why now?
Why would this happen now?

Why would part of you and part of me?
Happen now?
Now?
Of all of the times?
Now?

Everything is so crazy.
I missed the missed signs.
I didn't even think.

How am I supposed to do this?

I am all alone.
So alone.

Except, that's it, isn't it?
Now…
Until I do what I have to do,
I'm not alone,
Ever.

November 2023

I truly don't want to do this. That's what keeps going through my mind. I thought I wouldn't feel like this, but I guess you never know until it actually happens. Too many things have happened. I know he isn't right for me, he isn't right for himself, his own life. So, he can't be right for this either. Is this even real yet? Where does the line lie? If it is, it's not their fault.

All I ever wanted in my life was this, I'm blessed, and I've got to experience it before, in different forms and fonts. I'm so incredibly amazing at it. It could very well be my purpose and reason for this life. But, this person is wrong, the timing couldn't be worse. But what if it's not? And then I make a decision that isn't what's meant to be? How can I be sure?

November 2023

Aubrey Ann

My love
My darling

Dark hair, olive skin, green eyes
A sprinkle of freckles across her perfect nose
Smart and witty, caring and strong
Laughter that cuts the air
Like a warm summer breeze - comforting, relaxed
Bestest of friend, sweetest of sister

Crafted by love
Unhealthy and broken
But love all the same

I promise I'll remember your lesson
I promise to live by it
How could I not
I'll think about you every day
For the rest of my days

How do I truly resolve this
In my heart
My soul

You matter my love
You always will

I'm sorry, eternally sorry
I'll love you always
And forevermore

November 2023

two-seven

empty
disconnected
unfinished
reeling
mourning

a
piece
of
me
is
gone
forever

November 2023

12.01am

Honestly?

I don't know how I'll ever be okay again
On the outside
I'll keep going
Forever
I'll do it
But the core of me
Dying mangled mess
There is so much pain
Too much trauma
I don't even know where to start

December

                                                    not good.

January 2024

Unveiled Affair

6 years of secrets
Divulged
How do I say it
Why is writing it
Ink to paper
So much worse
Than saying it
I'm so angry
I'm so relieved
It wasn't me
I didn't ruin it
I'm free from the years of guilt
It is not my burden to carry
It his
Hers
Theirs
All of them

January 2024

?What I lost in the fire? What I gained from the fire?

How do I untangle a twisted rotting mess of emotions
Feelings, memories, trauma, and pain
Its spans months, reaches back into years and years
So many years you don't know who you really are or how you really got here

But you have to wake up every day and keep going, your kids need you
They rely on you, and they're looking up to you
Little eyes, gentle hearts, watching you handle this
Watching you not handle this

Upset because your nails broke after so long
So now your hands feel portly and ugly
But really, you're upset because your whole life feels like a lie
Because someone you loved and trusted and gave your life
Your soul and your body to, did the worst thing you could imagine

Your brain is trying to recalibrate every memory, feeling and milestone
The years of memories and experiences that shaped you
Into the person you are today
Are mistaken memories, feelings, and milestones
They aren't real

So how do you know who you actually are?

How do you untangle the web of betrayal?

January 2024

shatter

I am so broken
I thought it was bad before
The culmination
One after the other
Month after month
I want to fall apart
I feel so sad
So heartbroken
So rejected
So angry
Vast
Deep
Heavy
Chest cracking
I want to hide forever
Cry for eternity
I'm tired to my bones
Someone
Please
Look after me

Anyone

Help

January 2024

stop romanticising a version of him

and us

that you made up in your head and heart full of hope

February 2024

Embers Linger

So alone
But there are embers
Reminiscent of drama
Of people
Of love
Of pain
Pain that still lurks
Into the peripheries of my soul
Enough
The breaths aren't quite clear and deep
But the alone
It's so quiet

I tease on the edge of self-destruction
Do I want them?
Or drama?
Attention?
Or am I just lonely?

And that toxic love
Manipulates memories
Makes it seem like a viable option

I'm lonely
It's quiet
The pain lingers
I'm still trying to avoid it if I can
Embers

February 2024

Fated

I romanticised
Every relationship
Every person
Every possibility

In my mind
I turned it into
A beautiful novel
Everything integrated
Except for the truth
And reality

All because
I always wanted it to be worth something
So that there was a point to it all
A reason
A resolution for the pain

What if I'm meant to be alone
And I'm wasting a good and beautiful life
Wishing and hoping
For a love that isn't fated for me

I've lost so many people who are still breathing

And so much time on reality with no magic

March 2024

Admit the truth, Set me free

Why? That's what you ask me? So, I'll be honest, brutally honest. It's because I wish he would choose me, would have chosen me. Because I'm still feeling rejected and hurt and betrayed by the way he treated me, what I went through, by what we created and how I have been discarded for good by him. And it's not that I want 'him'. But I want those micro moments where I felt connected and felt love. A mirage, an oasis. Doubts fill the void; there is nothing else that will. Was it even ever real? Was it just my love reflected back from an empty vessel? That over those many, many months I had hope. And that hope built scenarios and dreams and futures that would never have happened anyway but they're still there. But it's done. It's really over. How do I get to the part where I'm actually set free? I want to scrub his memory from my mind, and from my body.

March 2024

Cursed

I never want to see him again

But

I look for him wherever I go

Answers

Does it matter who she is?
If it's the ex?
If it's the 'best friend'?
If it's the 24 year old hookup?
Will knowing what her eyes look like?
Make it easier to understand?
Why I got pain, and she gets pleasure?
Will knowing her story help to understand?
Why respect and care and love and commitment,
Were given to her and not to me?

March 2024

Reality

I didn't even know what you took from me
When I found out the truth
I didn't know the true cost of what I had lost

It's not what you think
It's not about you
What you did
It's about me

You didn't just inflict the worst betrayal
Or take my trust of others
Ashes to wind

You took my trust in me
My faith in my intuition
The flag on a hill
I spent 14 years dead and dying on

Proclaiming! Never, ever, ever!
Protecting, Forever and ever!

For you to then excise my insides
My literal flesh and blood

And now
I'm just supposed to eat breakfast
Pay bills, make jokes and feign normal?

March 2024

The 22nd

22nd of the month
Will you give me my reprieve

If I promise to let myself feel
The pain that swallows me whole
If I promise to be brave and face it
Let it consume me from my insides

Will I get my freedom
Will I get my peace

I'll bargain with anyone
Barter with the devil himself
If it's a guarantee that
I'll be finally and truly free

I'm letting their poison
Bury me alive

Tell me the remedy
I'll trade eternity's peace
To exit this one now
I Beg

March 2024

Haunted

I don't want to die
I promise

But

I'm so tired inside
I'm battling
Deep self-hatred

I just fucking wish
I didn't care

I'm literally made
Created
To Care
To Love
So why am I suffering
In loneliness

Relentlessly
Haunted

March 2024

Make it make sense

You stay in it.
You're with her.
She's 'better' than me.
You commit.
You don't look back.
I'm your villain.

You give her what I waited for.
What I begged for.
Bare minimum.
Respect.
Care.

Slow Transitions Begin

Mirrors

And

Maybe

Smoke

Or

Fire

April 2024

Fateful Delusion

Do the signs really mean anything?
Or is it hopeful delusion?
A sign in the stars!
The number revealed!
Again, and again!

The book you chose.
The page you opened.

It's only meaningful,
To the consequence you give it.

Emotion lingering,
Thoughts swirling.

Make meaning,
To feel a sense of control,
Of fate.

Like it could be written in the stars,
Destined by the moon.

Only the dreamers.

April 2024

I'm Wondering…

Would it matter if no one liked my words
That no one understood the rhyme
Would it be enough that I thought it was
That it made me feel like art

April 2024

Sea Through

Feel like there will never be true healing
Unless someone can actually see me
Actually love me
Does it matter if I do
Because I do
I see a magic that no one can
The care, heart, love
Emerald glistening eyes
Excited, playful
Freckles sunkissed
Salty waves in lengths and lengths of hair
From nature and gratitude
But to the world
I'm glass

April 2024

Virtuosity

Eternal dreamer
True love
Real love
All-consuming
Adventurous
Affection
Obsessive
Deep
Artistic
Adoration

April 2024

When I was…

It's unfair that the things
That make me, me
Are the things that broke me
   When I was 5
      When I was 7
         When I was 10
            When I was 14
               When I was 16
                  When I was 19
                     When I was 22
                      When I was 24
                       When I was 27
                      When I was 30
                     When I was 33
                    When I was 34
                     When I was 36

                      When I was 37

April 2024

Burn Off

You completed the labour
Surveyed the terrain
Took stock of the damage
The wildfire decimated

You watched and gave it time
Let the flames return to embers
The embers turn to charcoal
The rain came

It washed away
The rotten and the dead
Gave life to the residues
Little signs of hope and of calm
Seeking the light it deserves
To flourish once again

You tended to this land
Healing the ground
Protected the foundation

Burning containment lines
Insure, Ensure

And now
Another season
Is it wildfire season?

April 2024

Romanticised Fabrication

It's been months
But still
I log into a cloud fed screen
Checking again
For the tenth time today
For the 5th month this year
If you're waiting there too
Then I can lie to myself (I do every time)
Pretending we are looking at the same screen
Pretend though, that it's a moon we are gazing at
Romanticised fabrication
A sliding door in time
Or in the sky
Saying I love you back
Fool's daydream
Toxic habits

April 2024

Ask the question
Get the answer

Play stupid games
Win stupid prizes

May 2024

Modern Lust Story

Entice you through a screen
A witty prompt
A clever opener
Just enough attention
Just enough
To hook you in
Chasing dopamine
You're desperate enough to join the quest
But there is no Sunday night message
No Wednesday night dinner plans
You'll hear from them, maybe Thursday
"Sorry it took so long to reply, been so busy"
But you know just as well as I
That if they really wanted to try and see you
For all of you
You would never be left wondering

May 2024

Me Villain, You Hero

You were always trying to wrap things in the neatest bow
And you couldn't do that while it was obvious that you were
Manipulating
Using
Abusing
Controlling

You had to wait until you had broken me so badly
That I became
Distant
Sad
Untrusting
Pessimistic

Then
It was finally your opportunity

Me Villain, You Hero

Your ego prevails - your storyline suits
So then, I'm nothing
Discarded faster than scraps
You leave me alone, finally
I'm alone
Left
Alone

May 2024

just the two of us, just the three of us

Created together
Not merely in lust
No
It was far beyond lust
I don't regret my decisions
But that doesn't mean I don't grieve
It was real
I know it was her
I could sense her
I could feel her
I wasn't alone
In the car, in the shower, in the kitchen
In the dead of the night
Just the two of us
Just the three of us
You weren't really there though
So how would you understand
The pain of having to let go
Because of timing, because of circumstance
Because of who you are and how you treated me
And as soon as the task was completed
And once I was left
Empty, bleeding and alone
You left
For good
For Forever

I'll forget you, but I'll never forgive you

I'll forget you but I'll never forgive how you refused to let me go, even and always after you said you didn't want me.

I'll forget you but I'll never forgive how you dragged me back to you, no matter how many boundaries I staked shakily with my hands, firm in the dirt, trying to protect myself.

I'll forget you but I'll never forgive how you weaponised your own decisions and risks and blamed me and shamed me.

I'll forget you but I'll never forgive how you let me fall asleep next to you, tears streaming down my face, with your back to me, threatening to leave if I dare make a sound while I cried myself to sleep.

I'll forget you but I'll never forgive how you would only tell me you loved me when you were begging for me back, pleading with me to give you another, and another chance.

I'll forget you but I'll never forgive how you made me agree that buying me dinner was the same as contributing when I had to lose that part of me, of us.

I'll forget you but I'll never forgive the months you selfishly, purposefully, fraudulently and intentionally stole from me.

I'll forget you but I'll never forgive how when you had used up every inch of my body, my soul, my kindness, my patience, my love, my devotion, my faith, that you then discarded me and moved on with the next warm body willing to feed your ego.

I'll forget you but I'll never forgive how you waited until I couldn't survive anymore being myself, until I was broken beyond repair, unable to access my loving patient nature, to turn it all around just so you could leave with your reclaimed ego and pride, and say it was all because of me.

I'll forget you (even if I have to force it) But I'll never, ever, forgive you.

May 2024

Retribution

I want you to feel bad
Not be let off the hook
I want my pain to haunt you
Eternally torment you
You deserve never to feel peace
Only painful emotional terror
A lifetime of mental affliction
An eternity of suffering

May 2024

never, EVER, again

I'll never ever again
Let anyone take from me
What you did
So carelessly
So purposefully
And I hope
That the memory of me
And what you did to me
Haunts you
Endlessly
Relentlessly
That every time you feel content
Feel happy, feel joy, feel peace
It is violently interrupted
By the memories
Of my devoted love
My care, my gentle touch
Our electric chemistry

Every chance
Every understanding
Endless forgiving
And the sound of my crying
And the sight of my tears
And the pit in your stomach
That I know you wretchedly felt
Knowing that it was you
That twisted the knife
Dropped the bombs
Turned gold to dust
Then proclaimed
You were the victim

You'll be my lesson
And I'll be the memory
That terrorises you
To your dying breath

May 2024

Modern Courtship Revolution

It's not heartbreak
It's heartache
From a culmination
Not just the latest

We cosplay a couple
To feed a need
A quiet desperation
Then pretend it's fine to wake up and walk away
We don't talk about it
Don't dare speak about
How we walked the street, arms intertwined
An entire night folded into and around each other's bodies as we sleep
I don't dare whisper or allow the memory of how much it felt
When your hand so gently, carefully, lovingly brushed my hair back
Repeat sweeps of the soft baby hairs on my neck
The intimacy of that is so much more than the act

But!

It's not 1926 and romance is an imprisoned ghost
No second coming this time
So, then, we go back to our lives
Pretend all is fine
Add an ache to the pile of heartache
And carry on with tomorrow

May 2024

Alternate Reality

In an alternate lifetime
I'm awaiting your arrival
Anticipating
Dreaming
Olive skin
Emerald eyes
I would be counting down
Only six to go
Please arrive when you're supposed to
Because then you'll be here on my favourite
I didn't want to let you go
Not the part of you
That was a part of me
I think I'll always wonder
Are you waiting for me
Watching over me
I believe you are
My sweet
I'll see you at the end
Until then

The 26th of [stupid] May

(formally known as the 8th of stupid March)

Postmortem Withdrawn

I bled on these pages,
so I could stop bleeding in real life.

Mistaken for a post-mortem,
There was hope to heal all along.

The conclusion assumed,
Yet the narrative remains unwritten.

For now…

www.ingramcontent.com/pod-product-compliance
Lightning Source LLC
Chambersburg PA
CBHW020542080526
44583CB00013B/956